MW01520727

COL

1. Handicrafts -
   Fabrics + Yarn
2. Arts + Crafts

FABRICS & YARNS

Anne Coleman

Illustrated by
Malcolm S. Walker

Craft Projects

CLAY
FABRICS AND YARNS
NATURAL MATERIALS
PAPER AND CARD
SCRAP MATERIALS
WOOD

© Copyright 1989 Wayland (Publishers) Ltd

First published in 1989 by
Wayland (Publishers) Ltd
61, Western Road, Hove
East Sussex BN3 1JD, England

Editor: Hazel Songhurst
Designer: Kudos Services

British Library Cataloguing in
Publication Data
Coleman, Anne
     Fabrics and yarns.
     1. Textile handicrafts - Manuals - For
     children
     I. Title II. Series
     746
ISBN 1–85210–674–3

Printed in Italy by G. Canale & C. S.p.A. Turin
and bound in Belgium by Casterman S.A.

900666

FABRICS AND YARNS

Contents

Introduction

Materials and equipment

Collect pieces of fabric. Fabrics are made in different ways.

woven

knitted

felted

Before machines were invented, people worked by hand with threads and yarns, weaving and knitting them to make fabrics, then dyeing and printing the fabrics to add colour and pattern. Fabric was often decorated with embroidery, too. You can still see examples of this work in museums.

Today, although we have machines to make and decorate all our fabrics, many people still enjoy working by hand, making and decorating their own textiles. Fabric can be used like paint for making areas of colour and texture, and stitches make marks just like a pencil or crayon.

Look at the patterns

Look at the textures

spots

checks

big flowers

even

stripes

uneven

little

matt

stretchy

see-through

firm

hairy

rough

soft

shiny

smooth

Look at the colours

Sort your fabrics into colour groups and store them in plastic stacking boxes, plastic sacks or empty plastic sweet jars.

Collect yarns

All sorts of yarns for knitting, weaving and crochet and threads for embroidery and sewing are useful. You can even use ribbons and strips of fabric.

Keep yarns neat by winding them into balls or onto cones or pieces of card.

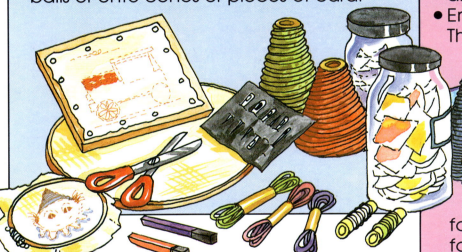

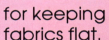

Always be on the look out for ideas for your textile pictures and patterns. Look at the shapes of flowers and trees or the patterns on rocks. Look at the shapes and patterns of buildings, vehicles and people. Ideas come from stories, music and drama. You can use the geometric shapes in maths and the patterns you see on pottery, metal, stone and wood. Collect pictures of the things made by hand by people from other countries Keep your pictures, ideas and experiments in a folder.

Other equipment

- Scissors. You need sharp scissors.
- Needles. You will need a variety to thread thick and thin threads.
- Embroidery rings. These are useful for keeping fabrics flat.
- Pins and tweezers.
- Water soluble fabric marker or chalk to draw out your design.
- Keep your equipment in a box or basket.
- Always take care to handle equipment sensibly.

Weaving

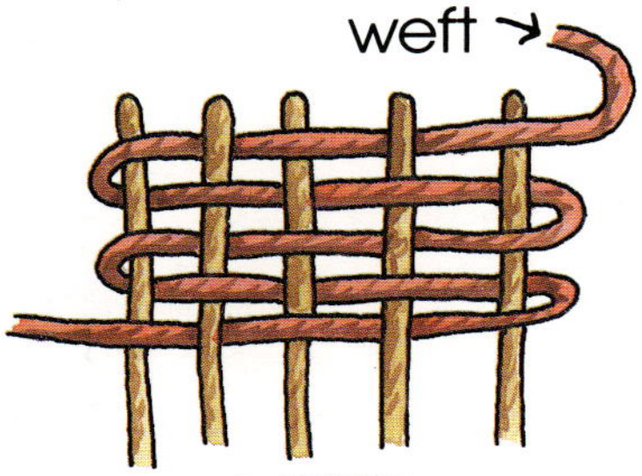

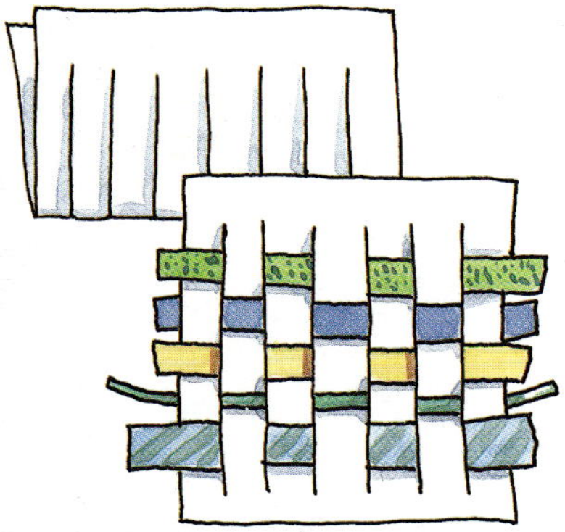

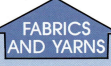

Many fabrics are woven on a loom. The **warp** threads are parallel to the edge of the fabric (selvage) and the **weft** threads are woven under and over the warp. The loom keeps the weaving taut. Practise by folding a sheet of paper in half and cutting slits in the folded edge. Open out and weave in strips of coloured paper. On the first row the strip should go over and under alternately. On the second line, it should go under and over alternately.

Different looms

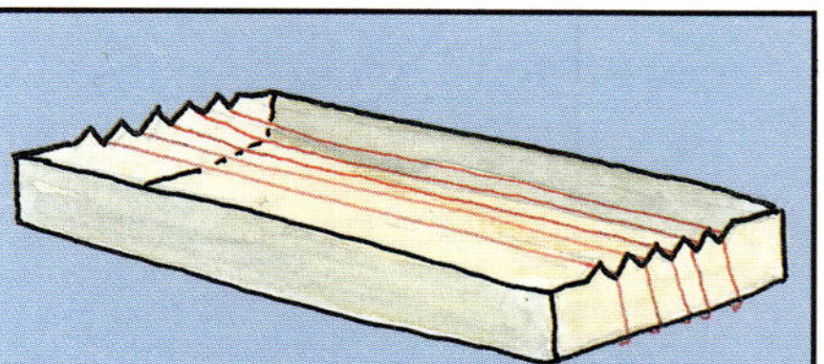

Shoe box loom: cut notches or slits across the ends and take the warp threads right round the box. Weave, then cut the warp across the back. Knot warp threads at top and bottom. **Old picture frame**: knock panel pins along top and bottom. Wind the warp threads round the pins. **Polystyrene dishes**: cover first with fabric to stop warp threads cutting through. Wind warp round the outside or sew it through.

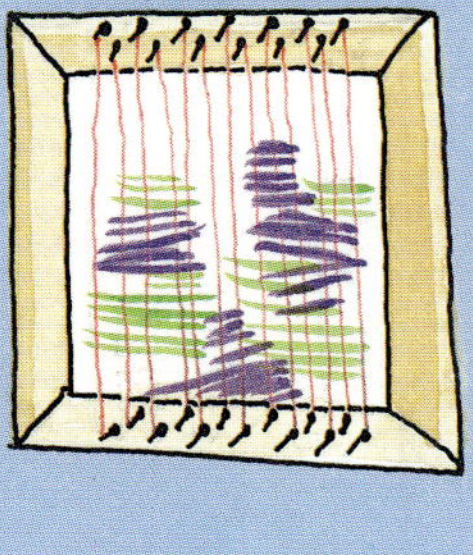

Making a cardboard loom

Use a piece of card about 15 cm x 10cm. Cut notches evenly along the top and bottom edges of the card. Wind fine string round the notches and across the front of the loom. Knot each end round the edge of the loom. These are the warp threads. You should have an odd number of warps. Using a variety of threads, yarns and strips of fabric, weave backwards and forwards across the warp. Weave each row in a slight curve, so that the weaving is not too tight. Push the weaving down firmly with your fingers or a fork. When you come to the end of the thread or want to change the colour, knot the end and push it to the back. Lift the weaving off the card. You can push a stick through the loops of the warp at the top and trim the bottom with fringes.

making fringes

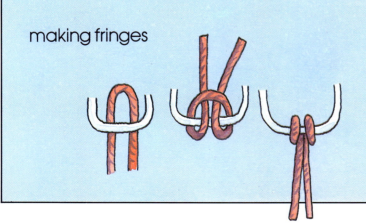

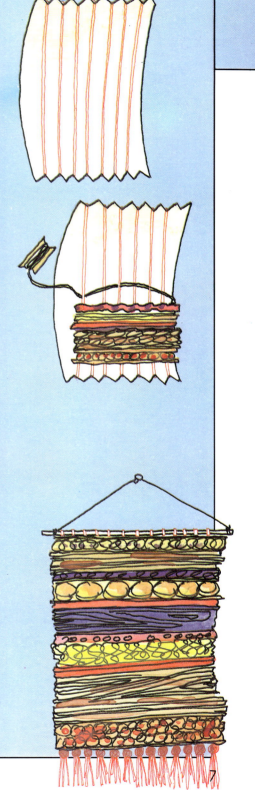

Make a woven ring

You will need

- 1 wooden ring (18 cm wide)
- 1 sharp needle
- 1 tapestry or weaving needle
- Double-sided sticky tape
- Beads
- Yarns: 9 x 32 cm lengths of strong, smooth double knitting wool or weaving yarn for warps. A variety of textured yarns for the weft.

More ideas

You can make a larger ring by using a metal lampshade ring or a hoop or even a bicycle wheel.

1. Knot 8 of the warps across the ring. A small piece of double-sided sticky tape will hold the yarn in position. Thread beads on to some warps.

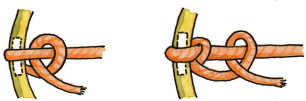

2. Knot the last warp to the ring. Take the other end to the middle and knot round all the other warps. You should have an odd number of warps (17). Cut the end off each, leaving 2 cm. Cover the ring by wrapping yarn round, trapping and securing the end of each warp as you go.

Shuttle

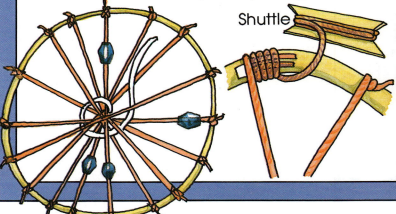

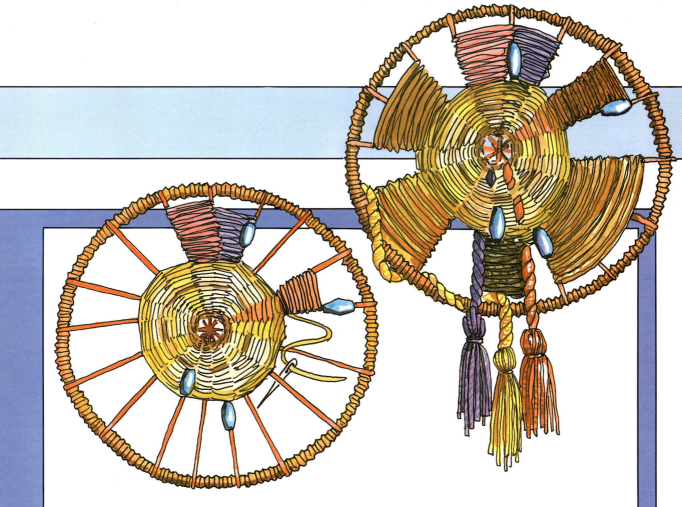

If you finish the yarn on the shuttle, secure the end by threading it through a sharp needle and pushing it back through the wrapping.

3. Thread the loose end of the last warp through a tapestry needle and start to weave round and round the centre. Weave with different textures or colours all the way round or just on two or three warps. Finish off by darning back through the weaving. Add a loop to hang up your weaving. Make tassels (p.23).

Shuttle

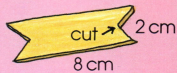

cut ↗ 2 cm

8 cm

Make a shuttle with stiff card 8 cm x 2 cm. Cut a notch in each end. Wind a smooth yarn round this.

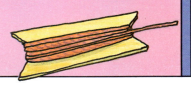

Colouring fabrics

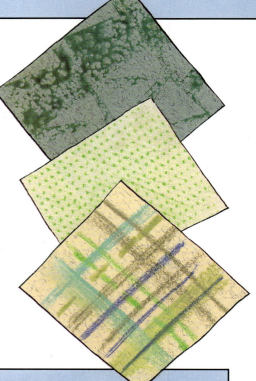

Many fabrics have a pattern printed on the surface. Look at your fabric pieces closely and see which are printed. You can colour and pattern fabrics yourself, using fabric crayons or paint. Choose fabric which is light coloured, so that the paints or crayons show up well. Bleached calico, silk, organdie, cotton polyester or poplin are suitable fabrics to use, but try colouring small pieces of a variety of fabrics to see which you like best. New fabric has stiffener added, called dressing, so it should be washed first in detergent and rinsed well.

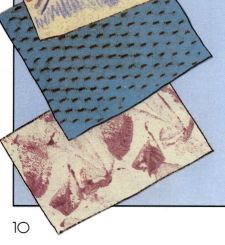

Direct fabric crayons

You can buy two kinds, one like pastel crayons and one like felt-pens. Try these separately or together . Pin the fabric to a drawing board and crayon straight onto it.

•Make marks: straight line patterns, zig-zag patterns, criss-cross patterns.
•Overlap colours like red and yellow, red and blue, blue and yellow. What new colours are

produced? What happens if you crayon over a coloured fabric? Notice how the colours change.

●Place a hard, textured material like rug canvas, wood grain, plastic mesh, under the fabric and make rubbings with the pastel crayon.

Direct fabric paints

These can be painted or printed straight onto fabric. Hold the fabric flat in a ring or pin it onto a frame. Try the paint on both wet and dry fabric. Pour some of the paint onto a piece of foam or felt in a saucer.

●Print patterns on the fabric with cork, sponge, crumpled paper or cut up potato dipped into the paint.

●Dip an old toothbrush into the paint and splatter onto the fabric with the end of a stick.

●Printing, painting or splattering can be done through a stencil cut in a piece of paper and laid over the fabric.

When the paint or crayon is dry, place the fabric face down on a piece of clean paper on an ironing board and iron carefully to fix it.

Collage

Sticking materials to a background is called collage.

You will need

- Sharp scissors for cutting fabric
- Glue which is specially made to stick fabrics and card, such as PVA glue
- A glue spreader or a curved needle. A cocktail stick can be used for dots of glue
- Tweezers are useful for placing fabric shapes in position
- A firm fabric background. Floppy fabric can be stiffened by:
  a. Sticking fabric to card, paper or polystyrene.
  b. Ironing iron-on interfacing to the back.
  c. Using paper backed hessian (sold as wallpaper).
- A variety of fabrics and threads, plaits, braids and fringes

Making pictures and patterns

Always choose fabrics which look right for your picture or pattern. Cut simple shapes which are big enough not to fall apart. Spread a little glue on the background and press the fabric onto the glue.

Making textures

Cut strips of fabric, spread on glue and roll them up. Fray out the edge of a strip of fabric, glue and roll. Cut into the edge of a strip of non-woven fabric like felt to make a fringe, glue and roll. Stick these textures down in patterns and to decorate pictures.

You can dip fabric in wallpaper paste, squeeze out the surplus and arrange the wet fabric on the background. Pleat and gather and swirl the fabric into patterns and textures.

More ideas

You can also cover a cardboard cone shape with glue-soaked fabric to create a figure. Natural fabrics like muslin, tarletan and hessian are good for this. Always allow a collage to dry thoroughly even if it takes several days.

Make a fabric collage

You will need

- Sharp scissors
- Tweezers
- 3 dishes or saucers
- PVA glue
- Yoghurt pot
- Glue spreader
- A piece of thin card about 30 cm x 20 cm
- Scraps of fabric in tones of one colour, from dark to pale
- Strips of fine fabric (muslin or tarletan)
- Yarns or string
- Pictures or your own drawings of fish

1. With sharp scissors, cut up the fabrics into small pieces. Divide between the three dishes.

pale   medium bright   dark

2. Draw the shape of the fish on the card. The drawing should be big enough to fill the card. Divide the shape into smaller areas, looking at the photo or drawing to help you.

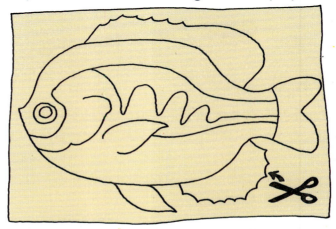

3. Spread glue in part of one area and press the fabric pieces onto the glue. Repeat until the area is filled.

4. Yarn and string make flowing lines. Spread glue along a line then press two, three or four lengths of yarn to it, close together.

5. Dip strips of fine fabric in PVA glue diluted with water. Place on the fins and tail and pleat and swirl. Leave to dry.

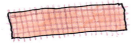 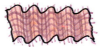

More ideas

Make two fish, one a mirror image of the other, cut them out and stick together to make a mobile. Get together with friends and make a shoal of fish.

Embroidery

Making patterns with stitches is embroidery. You can make marks on fabric with thread just as you can with a pencil on paper.

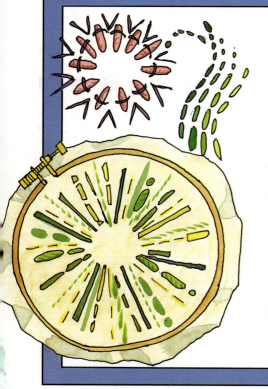

Choose a colour you like and collect together smooth yarns and threads all in that colour. You should have some pale and some dark as well as bright colours. Choose both thick and thin threads, shiny yarns, knitting yarns and sewing threads, embroidery cotton and even string. Make sure you have needles to fit each yarn. Choose a plain coloured background fabric which looks good with the threads. Woven fabrics are easier to work on. Try

More ideas

Make all sorts of patterns and textures with stitches: criss-cross, blocks of pattern, lines, circles. The same pattern looks different if you use different colours: all cream and white on a cream or white background, all black and grey on white, all white and cream on a dark background. Try out different colour schemes.

calico, crash, imitation linen. You could use a piece of curtain fabric or dress fabric. Put the fabric in an embroidery ring to hold it taut.

Thread one of your needles with a length of yarn about 30 cm. (If you use a very long piece of yarn, it tangles up. Try it and see). Start from the middle and make stitches spring outwards like fireworks. Use some of all the threads and try to make the stitches look dense and rich. Some thinner yarns can be embroidered on top of the thicker yarns. Use even and uneven stitches, big and small stitches.

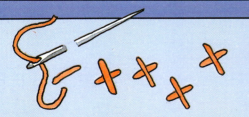

Straight stitch is easy. It will make all the patterns you see on these two pages.

Make a window picture

You will need

- A piece of card 19 cm x 17 cm
- Craft knife
- Ruler
- Pencil and felt pen
- Glue
- Double-sided sticky tape
- A piece of plain coloured fabric
- A variety of smooth yarns
- Needles and scissors
- Embroidery ring
- Picture of a view

Views

What can you see through a window? Landscape, buildings, sea, people, animals? What can you see looking into a window? Draw your ideas.

1. To make a window.
Use the craft knife and ruler to cut 1 strip of card from the 19 cm edge. Cut 2 strips of card from the 17 cm edge. Each strip should be 1 cm wide. Measure 2 cm in from each edge and draw a line to make a rectangle. Cut out.

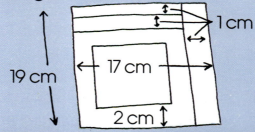

2. On the wrong side of the hole glue the strips across to make a window.

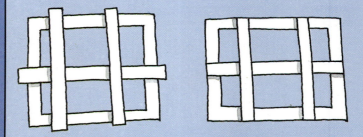

Trim. Turn it over. Draw a line round each section with a felt pen.

3. Iron the fabric and mark out a rectangle 15 cm x 12 cm with a fabric marker. Copy the outlines of your picture. You can trace it onto the fabric if you hold the fabric over the drawing up against a window. Put the fabric in an embroidery ring.

4. Fill the outlines of the shapes with stitches. Use the stitches to make lines, circles, explosions, whirls, blocks, and criss-crosses. Use long, short, even, uneven, spiky, smooth stitches.

Iron the back of the picture. Stick double-sided tape on the back of the frame. Press the frame onto the picture.

French knots make blobs and spots.

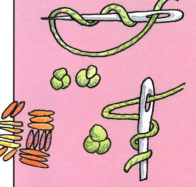

Add fabric paints, crayons, beads, sequins.

Using patterned fabrics

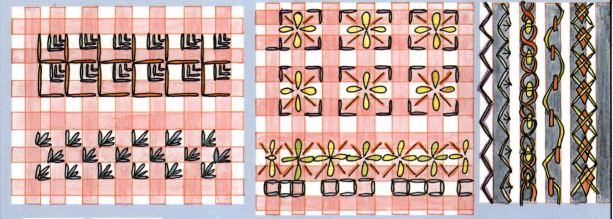

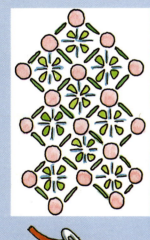

1.

2.

chain stitch

You can decorate patterned fabrics with stitches. Use a bought fabric or a patterned fabric you have printed yourself. It is easy to make patterns on striped, checked, spotted and regular designs. You can plan on paper by drawing with a thick, highlighting marker pen, then decorate the patterns with a felt pen. The pattern on the fabric should be big enough for your stitches. Try dark stitches on light fabric, or light on dark, or use another tone of the same colour. You can also decorate big shapes printed on fabrics, like leaves and flowers. Use smooth threads and a sharp needle.

Using mesh fabrics

There are many mesh fabrics, like canvas, which can be used as a background for stitches. Rug canvas has a large mesh and you can use strips of fabric and ribbon as well as thick yarns. Other types of canvas have a smaller mesh and need thinner threads. You can also colour canvas with paints or crayons. If you do, remember to iron the colour to fix it. Because the mesh is even, you can make patterns by counting the lines and spaces of the canvas.

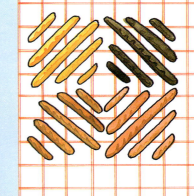

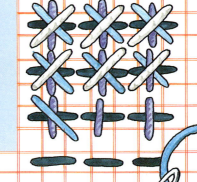

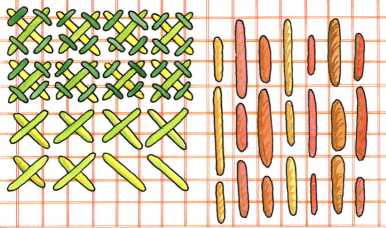

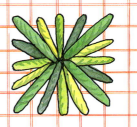

blunt tapestry needle

Bind the edges of the canvas with masking tape before beginning. Work with a blunt tapestry needle.

Make a mask

You will need

- A mesh
  vegetable bag
  big enough to fit
  over your head
  NOT POLYTHENE
- A large blunt
  needle (tapestry
  or weaving)
- Crochet hook
- A variety of
  knitting and
  weaving yarns:
  All white for a
  ghost
  All green for
  camouflage
  All glitter for a
  festival
  All stripes for a
  tiger or a wasp

1. If the mesh bag is too big, machine or handsew tightly up one side and cut off the spare fabric. The bottom edge should come to the tip of your nose. Ask someone to mark the position of your eyes with two pieces of knotted thread.

2. Put the bag over a football or a piece of card to hold the mesh taut. Make the eyes by couching (oversewing a thick yarn) round and round the mesh.

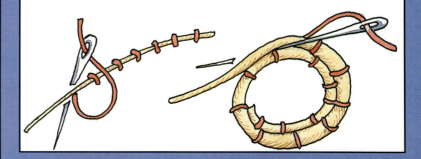

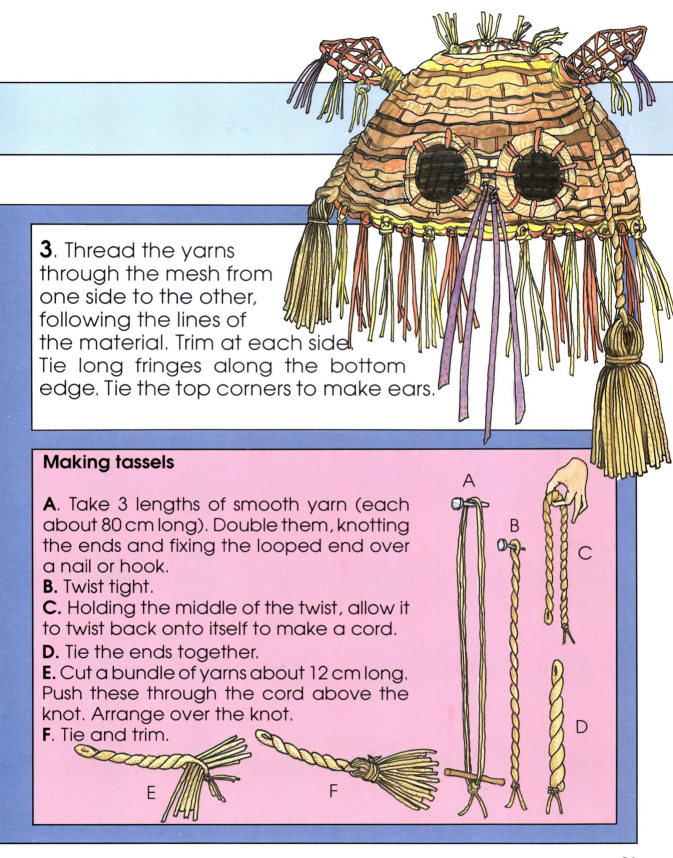

3. Thread the yarns through the mesh from one side to the other, following the lines of the material. Trim at each side. Tie long fringes along the bottom edge. Tie the top corners to make ears.

Making tassels

A. Take 3 lengths of smooth yarn (each about 80 cm long). Double them, knotting the ends and fixing the looped end over a nail or hook.

B. Twist tight.

C. Holding the middle of the twist, allow it to twist back onto itself to make a cord.

D. Tie the ends together.

E. Cut a bundle of yarns about 12 cm long. Push these through the cord above the knot. Arrange over the knot.

F. Tie and trim.

Appliqué

Making a template

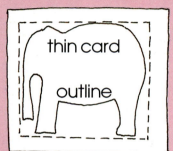

thin card

outline

Use thin card and sharp scissors. Draw a rectangle which is roughly the size you want. Draw the shape so that it fits into the rectangle, touching the edges. It is always best to draw from life if you can and not from other drawings.

Sewing on fabric shapes is called appliqué. You can cut out fabric shapes and sew them onto a background either by hand or using a sewing machine. Draw the shapes onto the fabric with fabric marker and cut out. You might find it easier to make a template with card that can be used several times.

Shapes for appliqué should be as simple as possible. Add details with stitches. Use any firm background. Tack flimsy fabrics onto another fabric, like calico. The patterns and colours of the background and shapes all affect each other. Some look better together than others. Make a chart of how colours and patterns react and keep it for reference. Remember, you can print or colour your own fabric.

To hold the shapes in place for sewing:

1. Pin and tack **or**
2. Stick with a very small amount of fabric glue **or**
3. Iron on a small piece of bondaweb between the shape and the background.

Sew on the shape with small running stitches either all or part the way round. Decorate with different kinds of stitches.

A little padding will make the shape stand out.
You can use knitted and hand-knitted fabrics as well as woven and felt fabrics.

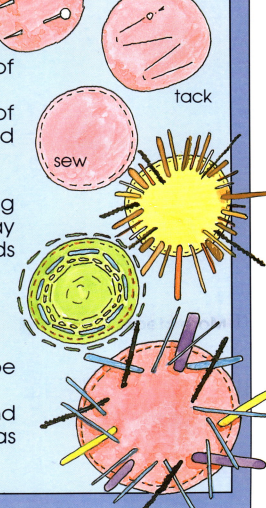

pin

tack

sew

Using a sewing machine

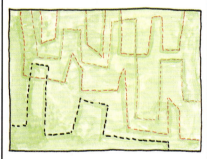

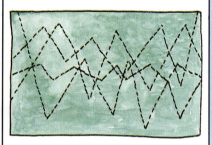

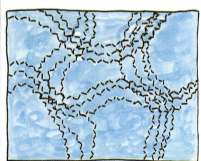

Sewing machines are useful and easy to use, even for a beginner.

Be careful to keep your fingers away from the needle and drive as evenly as possible. Learn to thread the machine and wind the bobbin evenly. Ask someone to help you. Learn to machine stitch by making patterns on pieces of calico, cotton or poplin backed with iron-on vilene. Use straight stitch or zig-zag or combine them. Make interesting freehand patterns from one side to the other and from top to bottom. Start and finish at an edge if possible. Cut off threads close to the edge. Make straight, curved and zig-zag line patterns from side to side and criss-crossing.

To make a sharp turn, lift up the machine foot with the needle in the fabric. Turn the fabric and set the foot down again.

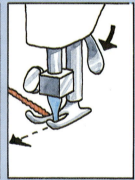

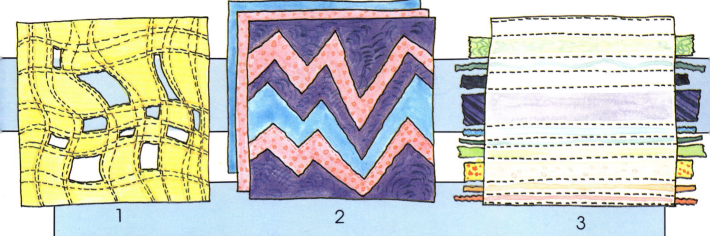

1   2   3

Other materials to use

1. Use a close, zig-zag stitch to make a criss-cross pattern. Cut out some of the shapes inside the stitch line.

2.   Use   three   pieces   of different-coloured   woven   fabric tacked   together.   Machine   a pattern, then cut away the top or top two layers inside the stitch lines of some of the shapes.

3. Use a layer of see-through fabric tacked onto a layer of cotton or calico. Machine parallel lines from one side to the other, using the foot as a guide. Thread yarn or strips of fabric   through   the   channels between the stitches.

Appliqué

You can attach fabric shapes by machining round them, but this is sometimes difficult, so machine a pattern right across, perhaps with parallel lines or with a criss-cross pattern. The stitches will hold the fabric shapes in place.

27

Make a quilted pencil case

You will need

- 2 rectangles of cotton or calico 20 cm x 25 cm
- A piece of terylene wadding 20 cm x 25 cm
- Bias binding
- 2 snap fasteners

You can make bags by folding a rectangle in two or three, or by joining two rectangles. Make a paper pattern first. If you use plastic for one layer, the bag will be waterproof. Use appliqué or embroidery on the top layer.

1. Make a sandwich with two pieces of calico and one piece of wadding as the filling. Tack the layers together.

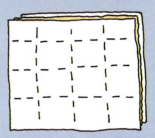

2. Quilt, by machining up and down and across the middle. Trim the leftover threads to about 3 mm. Make a pattern with machine stitches, starting and finishing at the edges. Use the machine foot as a guide. Pull out the tacks.

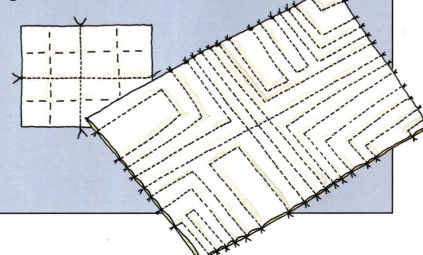

3. Using fabric pastels or felt fabric pens, fill in some of the spaces between the stitches. You can plan this on paper first if you like. Iron, to fix the colour.

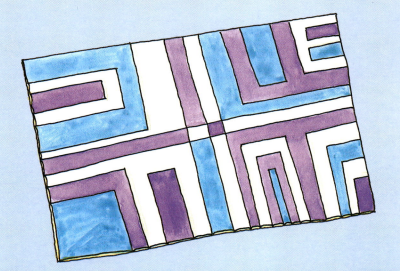

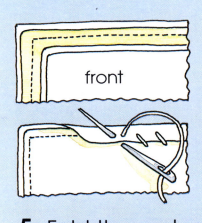

front

4. Bind the edge of the quilting to neaten it. Open the bias binding along one edge. Put the edge to the edge of the quilting and machine along the groove. Turn the binding to the back and hem down.

5. Fold the rectangle into three. Pin and oversew the edges. Sew on the snap fasteners.

Glossary

Bias binding A non-fraying strip of material used to bind the edge of fabric.

Bobbin The piece inside a sewing machine round which the thread is wound.

Bondaweb A strip of material that sticks to fabric when it is ironed on.

Couching stitch Oversewing a thick yarn with thread to hold it in place.

Darning Crossing or inter-woven stitches sewn close together, often used to mend holes or tears.

Dressing The stiffener applied to new fabrics.

Fixing Patterns and colours made by fabric paints and crayons may come off unless they are 'fixed' or 'made fast' by ironing.

Machine foot The part of a sewing machine that holds the fabric in place beneath the needle.

Running stitch Short, neat straight stitches, used to fasten two pieces of material together.

Selvage The non-fraying edge of a piece of fabric.

Shuttle In weaving, the weft thread is wound round the shuttle which is then pushed through the warp threads.

Tacking stitch Long, loose, straight stitches used to hold material in place and usually taken out once the material is properly fastened.

Vilene A stiff material that can be ironed on to flimsy fabric to make a firm backing.

Warp In weaving, the threads that run parallel to the selvage.

Weft In weaving, the threads woven across at right angles to the warp threads.

Notes for parents and teachers

Fabric is an exciting, colourful and versatile medium which is easy to use for creative activity at home and in school. At home, scraps of material are easily found and, from an early age, children enjoy making fabric collages, simple sewing and other similar activities. Older children who have mastered tools and techniques, take pleasure in designing and making by themselves. With help and encouragement, activity with fabrics and yarns is an interest which can develop in many directions and one which can last a lifetime.

Creative work with fabrics and yarns in school gives an added dimension to art and craft. Many aspects of textiles can also be linked with science and technology.

Children should be encouraged to discuss and expand upon the ideas presented in this book. They should also be given every opportunity to try out their own ideas and designs and to choose their own materials. They need both freedom to experiment with stitch patterns, techniques and materials and also the experience of making their own templates and cutting out their own fabric shapes. Accurate sewing and cutting only comes with practise.

It is helpful to plan a scheme of work for textiles throughout the school to fit in with the curriculum. Each child should have the chance to try out different materials and techniques.

This book only touches upon some of the many aspects of creative textiles. Other ideas can be found in books on embroidery, knitting, weaving, fabric printing and so on. Many museums have sections devoted to textiles, as well as lively and interesting exhibitions.

Further information

A water soluble fabric marker is useful for drawing out designs which can be rubbed off with cold water. Embroidery rings keep fabric taut and prevent stitches pulling. Canvas stretchers can also be used: pin on fabric with drawing pins. Do read instructions on all fabric paints and crayons. When fixing, protect ironing board and work with newspaper. Children are often capable of using a sewing machine by eight, under supervision. They often work well in twos.
Starting and finishing should be firm. Start with a knot. Finish by weaving in and out of stitches at the back.

Index

900666